IMAGES
of America

FREEPORT

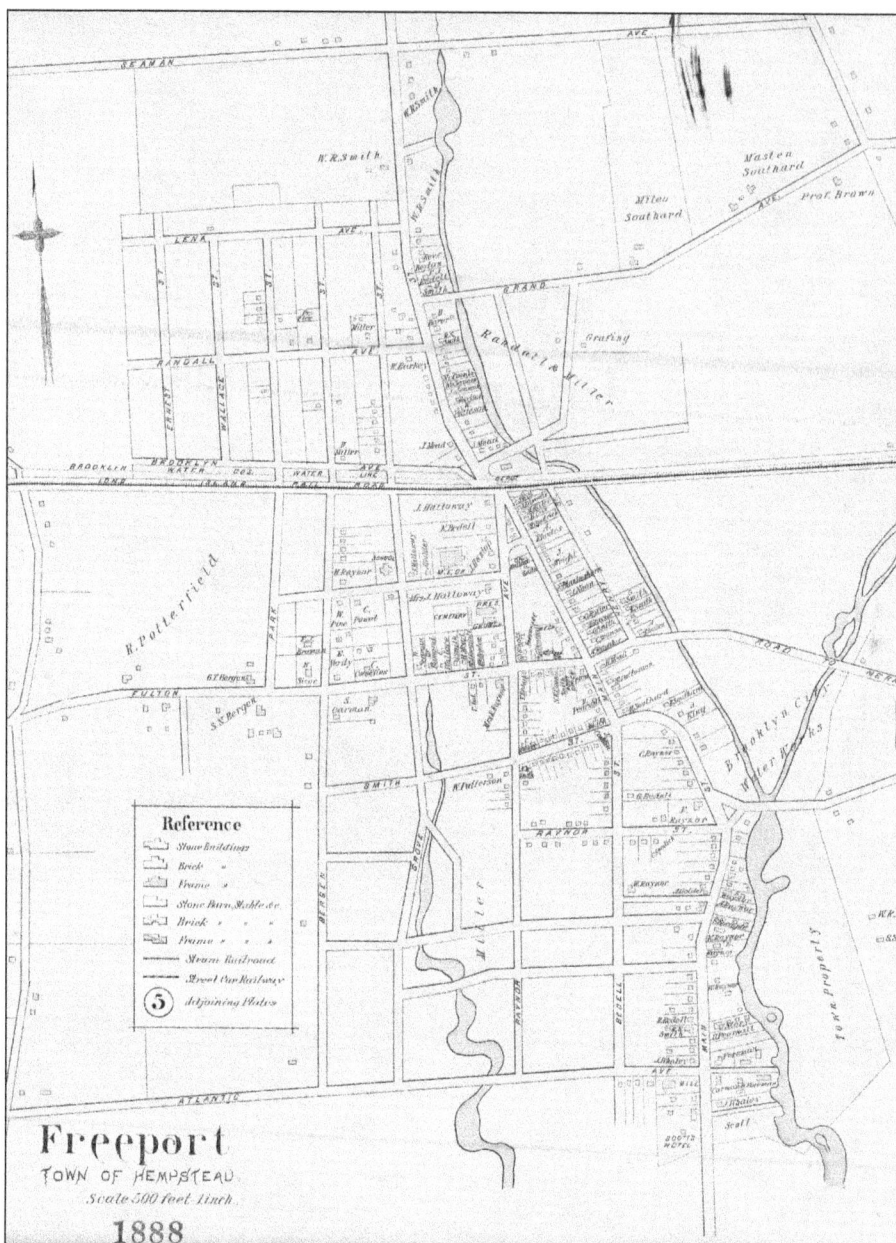

Reference

Stone Buildings
Brick "
Frame "
Stone Barn, Stable &c.
Brick "
Frame " . . .
Steam Railroad
Street Car Railway
(5) Adjoining Plates

Freeport
TOWN OF HEMPSTEAD
Scale 500 feet 1 inch.

1888

This 1888 map shows the boundaries of Freeport before it was incorporated. The hamlet extended to Seaman Avenue to the north and just below Atlantic Avenue to the south. The west boundary was Milburn Creek, and the east was Freeport Creek. Most of the houses and stores centered on or near Main Street. The City of Brooklyn owned considerable property near the railroad as well as on the Freeport Creek. (Freeport Historical Society.)

ON THE COVER: The Merokee Canoe Club was off the "anchored" home of Commodore Dexter Haight at 330 Branch Avenue. Johnson brothers Albin and Hilbert were members among the many young people. The club held popular water sports including canoe races, tilting races, and swimming races. Most of its activities were held on Randall Bay near the South Shore Yacht Club. (Freeport Historical Society.)

IMAGES
of America

FREEPORT

Cynthia J. Krieg and Regina G. Feeney

ARCADIA
PUBLISHING

Published by Arcadia Publishing
Charleston, South Carolina

Library of Congress Control Number: 2011941050

For all general information, please contact Arcadia Publishing:
Telephone 843-853-2070
Fax 843-853-0044
E-mail sales@arcadiapublishing.com
For customer service and orders:
Toll-Free 1-888-313-2665

Visit us on the Internet at www.arcadiapublishing.com

Dedicated to all those who have collected, preserved, and made
available the history of Freeport. You have inspired us to do the same.

CONTENTS

ACKNOWLEDGMENTS

The idea for this book grew out of a partnership between the Freeport Historical Society and the Freeport Memorial Library. In the fall of 2004, the library was invited to join Long Island Memories's digitization initiative sponsored by the Long Island Libraries Resources Council (www. longislandmemories.org). The library began by scanning the Freeport Historical Society's extensive postcard collection. Other collections soon followed. This collaboration has made historical material related to Freeport more accessible to all generations. As the site grew, we were often asked about writing a book on the history of Freeport. After adding more than 4,000 images and six newspaper titles to the digital site, we were ready to take on a new challenge.

This endeavor would have been impossible without the help and support of the Freeport Historical Society's vast photographic collection and its many volunteers. We would specifically like to thank Kerri Allegretta, Patrice Benneward, Jeanne Booth, Miguel Bermudez, Isabelle Drach, Nancy Feeney, Marty Himes, and Carol Poulos. The resources in the Long Island Room Collection, located at the Freeport Memorial Library, proved invaluable. We would also like to thank the staff at Arcadia Publishing, especially Erin M. Rocha and Abby Henry.

All photographs in this book come from the Freeport Historical Society unless otherwise noted by letter codes after each caption. We would like to thank the following organizations and individuals for allowing use of images from their collections: Kenneth Alcorn (KA), Baldwin Historical Society (BHS), Miguel Bermudez (MB), Cradle of Aviation (CA), Mary Cummings (MC), Peter Dilg (PD), Regina Feeney (RF), Freeport Memorial Library (FML), Ward Frost Jr. (WF), Marty Himes (MH), Library of Congress (LC), Donald Lowe (DL), Cynthia Krieg (CK), Rev. Dr. Eric C. Mallette (EM), University of Washington (UW), and the Village of Freeport (VOF).

INTRODUCTION

Freeport, or as it was originally called, "Raynor South," and later, "Raynortown," was founded about 1659 by Edward Raynor, after he came from Hempstead village. As the cow keeper, he brought cattle to the "spacious meadows and marshlands." He was drawn to the Great South Woods with its beautiful streams, well supplied with fish, flowing to a bay that yielded more fish. Escorted by Raynor on the trails he had blazed as a cow keeper, other pioneers followed. Most of them settled in log cabins on South Main Street.

The original first settlers were the Native American Merokes who found Milburn Creek to be a favorite stream. Besides boasting plenty of trout, it became one of the biggest wampum factories. On the north side of Seaman Avenue near the Kissing Bridge, arrowheads and other relics were found, indicating a fairly large encampment.

Little is known about the first 150 years of the settlement, but one event of importance was the visit of Pres. George Washington in the spring of 1790. By 1838, the hamlet consisted of about 40 dwellings that were centered on both sides of Main Street. Most residents were farmers or fishermen.

In Colonial days, Raynor South was known as a "free port" by seafarers. The legend is that boat captains landed their cargo to avoid the taxes charged for bringing goods into New York City or Sag Harbor. More likely, since there were no waterways large enough for big ships to dock, smaller local boats used dock space that local baymen provided without having to pay a fee. In 1853, the residents voted to change the name to Freeport.

During the Civil War, about 40 Freeporters joined the battle, and 14 did not return. Two of them were Mott brothers Dandridge and Joseph. A monument in their memory is now located on the grounds of the Freeport Historical Society. The Grand Army of the Republic Post No. 527 was named for Dandridge. After the war, there were still only 122 homes of farmers, fishermen, and local businessmen.

Many of the first real changes came with the arrival of the South Side Railroad in 1868. The train brought out "city" people who built summer cottages and created a need for such improvements as paved roads, electric lighting, and police. A referendum in 1892 decided the issue of incorporation. Soon after, when the Grove Street School burned down, the village government established the fire department, water department, and a power plant. The structure of the government established at that time is the same today, consisting of a president (now mayor) and four trustees.

In the Gay Nineties era, John J. Randall and his partner William G. Miller increased their real estate acreage by filling the lowlands with dirt from the bottom of man-made canals. Woodcleft Canal and Randall Bay are examples of these canals. Other businessmen flocked to Freeport and established banks, construction companies, insurance agencies, and real estate concerns. Notable among them were Lewis Ross, Charles Sigmond, T.C.P. Forbes, William Foreman, and George Wallace.

Before the turn of the 20th century, Freeport was famous for its oysters, which were shipped all over the world. The City of Brooklyn purchased many of the local ponds to supply water for its citizens. Oysters require a rare combination of both fresh and salt water to thrive. So this salinity was adversely affected when Brooklyn pumped out the water, and the oyster industry went into a decline.

Hotels, on or near the waterfront, sprung up, and Freeport became a popular resort. A 200-room hotel overlooked Woodcleft Canal, with a beach and a bathhouse. Amusement parks, hotels, inns, and other popular bathing beaches were responsible for bringing the rich and famous to the area. Trips by ferry to outlying Point Lookout, Nassau-by-the-Sea, the Greenhouse, and High Hill were popular summertime activities. The waterfront also attracted people to the South Shore Yacht Club and, later, the Freeport Yacht Club.

Show-business people found Freeport a perfect place to relax, and many, including Tom Smith (father of aviatrix Elinor Smith), Leo Carrillo, and Victor Moore, built homes. Over 500 actors called Freeport their summer home in this period. They formed the actors' organization that became world famous. The Long Island Good Hearted Thespian Society (LIGHTS) built its clubhouse on Fairview Avenue, and its members often gave far-reaching publicity to Freeport when they mentioned the village in their stage shows. Some of these members included Will Rogers, John Philip Sousa, Gentleman Jim Corbett, Al Jolson, Richard and Alf Ringling of the Ringling Bros. Circus, Flo Ziegfeld, and Irving Berlin. Later, showbiz personalities, who lived in Freeport, were Gabriel Heatter and Guy Lombardo.

Freeport had early ties to the fledgling airplane industry. Augustus Herring and Charles Manly, both innovators in flight, summered here. The Heinrich brothers manufactured airplanes for the US government. Freeport even had its own airport down at East Point. Elinor Smith, the famous aviatrix, grew up here.

In the 1920s and 1930s, Freeport's population grew as people considered it a year-round residence. Freeport had much to offer including a superior school system, churches of all denominations, and a vibrant business community. Spectacular houses as well as middle-income housing, found on tree-lined streets, were readily available. For recreation, there were theaters that featured vaudeville and movies, gun clubs, tennis clubs, canoe clubs, parks, restaurants, and golf courses. Playland Park, a miniature Coney Island, brought many visitors into the village. The Freeport Memorial Library, built as a war memorial in 1924, was a welcomed addition. Village hall was constructed as a replica of Independence Hall, and the post office is a magnificent Colonial Revival building.

During the 1920s, until the repeal of Prohibition, Freeport was a hot spot for rumrunners. Their boats were built here, as well as the Coast Guard cutters that chased them. Many of the baymen and restaurateurs were actively involved in the illegal liquor trade.

In the 1930s, the municipal stadium was built as a recreation center for high school football games, graduations, Memorial Day services, and semiprofessional baseball. Later, it hosted motorcycle and midget-car races. In 1930, the boundaries of the village were extended south to the bay.

Freeport today is a wonderfully diverse community that celebrates its rich and varied history. It is a mecca for fishing, both sport and commercial. The Nautical Mile (Woodcleft Avenue) is a working port with docks and a summer destination for tourists. The institutions that were put in place years ago still play an important role in the lives of its citizens, including our own police department and volunteer fire department.

One

SETTLEMENT TO INCORPORATION

Raynor's mills stood on Mill Road between Horsfall's pond and Freeport Creek in the 1870s. One was a sawmill and the other a gristmill, supplied by water from the pond. The property was sold in 1874 by Daniel Raynor to Isaac Horsfall, who upgraded the machinery and then sold the property to the Brooklyn City Water Department in 1885. The gristmill was torn down around 1926.

The oldest house in Freeport, also known as Bell Oaks, was built by Jacob Bedell around 1795 at Ocean Avenue and Randall Avenue. Five years later, the structure was moved east several hundred feet to a location at the northeast corner of Randall Avenue and Main Street. It was the home of R.H. Mayland, who was a major influence in the fire department.

The Powell homestead is located at 137 Babylon Turnpike and was built in the late 1700s. His farm extended from Babylon Turnpike to Columbus Avenue and from Grand Avenue to Seaman Avenue. Tiny windows over the rear door indicate the attic was used for bedrooms. John B. Powell was a farmer and, later, handled many road contracts for the village. His grandson John Pettit Powell (1850–1917) sold the house in the early 1900s.

William Rock Smith ("Daddy Bill") owned this ice pond, which was located on the east side of North Main Street, just south of East Dean Street. In the days before artificial ice was made, people cut ice in the pond and packed it in sawdust for use in the summer. Smith also built schooners here and transported them down to Freeport Creek on rollers. The journey took four days.

The Daniel Raynor homestead was located on South Main Street opposite Mill Road and was built in 1783. This farmhouse was a 2.5-story, cedar-shake structure. Judge Hilbert Johnson, village historian, and the Freeport Historical Society planned to preserve the building as a museum. World War II, lack of insurance coverage, and the fierce late-summer hurricane of 1944 led to this historic structure's demise.

Daniel Tredwell's (1826–1921) family home was on the north side of Merrick Road just east of Brookside Avenue. He began to practice law in 1848 and became Brooklyn's oldest lawyer. A historian, he wrote on a variety of subjects including the Civil War, lace, the sea, biographies, and the illuminating of books. He also wrote *Personal Reminiscences of Men and Things on Long Island*.

The Kissing Bridge is located on Seaman Avenue spanning Milburn Creek on the Baldwin border. The legend said that a Native American maiden of the Massapequa tribe met a man of the Iroquois tribe at this site. The Massapequa jilted lover of the Massapequa maiden crept up and dispatched the Iroquois Indian with his tomahawk. In later years, the bridge became known as a trysting place.

Raynor Rock Smith's homestead was located on East Merrick Road where Freeport meets Merrick around 1880. Raynor Rock Smith was a ship salvage master before the establishment of the US Life Saving Service. George B. Smith, hotel and restaurant owner and a son of Captain Smith, is holding his son George at left. T. Benson Smith and Charles S. "Tod" Power are also in the family group.

In January 1837, the *Mexico*, a sailing barque, wrecked in freezing weather off Long Beach. Freeporter Capt. Raynor Rock Smith, with his sons, dragged his boat from Raynortown and across the bay to aid the people on the boat. The Raynors were able to rescue eight. Tragically, 112 perished, most of them Irish immigrants. This monument on the Rockville Centre Lynbrook border marks their mass grave.

This crude wooden bridge on Mill Road spanned the millrace at Raynor's gristmill south of Horsfall's Pond. It was one of the few crossings of the East Meadow Brook. Wagon drivers would turn off the road to cool their horses by letting them wade into the pond for a drink. A 32-foot-wide reinforced concrete span replaced it in 1913.

A small two-story farmhouse was built at 43 Mill Road before the Revolutionary War and was probably owned by Joseph Raynor and his son Thomas. Over the centuries, a large addition was attached. The firehouse to the left was located on the east side of Bedell Street near Smith Street and Southside Avenue and was constructed in 1894. It was the first structure of Ever Ready Hose Company No. 1.

The Reverend Charles Boynton lived in this house on North Main Street. A former pastor of the Presbyterian church, he resigned because did not want to take a salary, and the congregation would not agree. The house was constructed of lime bricks, which he made from oyster shells in kilns he built. The walls were double layered with air spaces between, and it was dubbed the "warmest house on Long Island."

The Whaley house is located at 380 South Main Street near Atlantic Avenue and the Freeport Creek. James Whaley is sitting on a chair in front of the house. The farm extended from Main Street west, and the road through was known as Whaley's Lane, which later became Atlantic Avenue. Whaley family members were also involved in the fishing and boating trade.

Originally located at 170 South Main Street, this house dates back to about 1855. Mott Raynor (b. 1828) built the house on the farm of his father, Daniel. The top of the chimney was tilted 18 inches on the theory that witches could never fly down a crooked chimney. The home was moved in 1972 to 77 Bedell Street because of the fear of its demolition.

The Mott Monument was dedicated to two Freeport brothers, Dandridge and Joseph Mott, who died in the Civil War in 1864. Dandridge was killed by a sharpshooter, and Joseph died in a prison camp. The Dandridge Mott Post of the Grand Army of the Republic dedicated this monument to them. It is now located in the backyard of the Freeport Historical Society.

Two

WATERFRONT

Capt. William Patterson's oyster house was located on Freeport Creek. As oysters were harvested by the crew, they piled them around the inside walls of the oyster house. Some men culled the oysters for washing and then put them in a hatchway in the floor. They were washed with fresh water from a well and were barreled for shipment by railroad to the Fulton Fish Market in New York and Philadelphia markets.

Capt. Abe Smith's Oyster House stood on Hanse Avenue's west side near Mill Road in Turk's Island. In 1934, this aging structure was moved across Freeport Creek to the mostly undeveloped east bank from the west bank where it had many neighbors in the same business as its own. The house was moved when the Town of Hempstead agreed to widen Freeport Creek.

Elderly baymen (from left to right) Furman Seaman, Capt. John Whaley, William E. Golder, Capt. Tip Smith, Capt. Abe Smith, Police Chief John Hartmann, and Oliver Smith gathered around the stove to chat at Capt. Abe Smith's Oyster House. His friends, the Sunset Club, came to an annual birthday party on February 27. Captain Abe prepared the meal, and afterward, the men told old yarns.

Oysters were an important industry in Freeport; however, by the turn of the 20th century, as the surface level of the streams sank because of the Brooklyn Water Works, the business went into decline. Oysters thrive best on hard bottom areas in brackish bays, coves, and mouths of rivers, where there is land drainage to provide food and the waters are partially salty.

The *Empire State* dredge gouged out Old Freeport Creek, making it more navigable for large freight boats. It was deepened to 16 feet at low water and widened to an average of 200 feet. The creek was straightened and deepened to be an eastward line through Fighting Island and South Cow Meadow. The fill was used to build the Meadowbrook Causeway to Jones Beach.

19

Catboats on the Great South Bay were common from the 1880s to 1920s. They had an unusually wide beam and a comparatively small free board. They looked like a big saucer. The single mast was stepped far forward and carried the mainsail. The draft was shallow, and the catboats carried a centerboard. They were "homey, safe, and comfortable" but were slow and hard to handle.

A steam launch operates from a ship or a small boat and is typically used for short trips. Many actors and other residents of Freeport owned these launches, such as the *Virginian*, which were used for cruising nearby canals and bays. One such owner was William Furst, who was the musical director of the Empire Theater and a composer who had a summer home on Ocean Avenue.

RANDALL'S CHANNEL, FREEPORT, LONG ISLAND, N.Y.

In 1907, John J. Randall built a large channel from the Bayview section to Baldwin Bay. Randall Bay is 300 feet wide and 10 feet deep at low tide. On its shores were the South Shore Yacht Club; Beau Rivage; private homes, such as Victor Moore's; and the Casino. The fill from the channel allowed him to develop housing lots in the area west of the waterways.

The Woodcleft Canal was constructed in 1898 by John J. Randall and William G. Miller. It opened up a waterway directly into the South Bay. It was the first artificial waterway to the South Bay. Its channel was 100 feet wide and 10 feet deep at low tide. Steamers from the beach found accessible dockage, and owners of boats built boathouses along the shores.

Freeport Point Shipyard was founded by Fred and Mirto Scopinich just after World War I. They built more than 30 rumrunners and 15 Coast Guard boats. The Coast Guard boats ran at 26 miles per hour, while the rumrunners did 30 miles per hour, fully loaded. From 1937 on, the shipyard built small boats for the US and British navies, including air-sea rescue boats that could rescue pilots from planes downed at sea.

The Silver Wave Hotel was owned by Otto St. George and was located on the Little Swift Creek. It was a cozy restaurant with a full mahogany bar and was the headquarters for both bootleggers and revenue agents. Federal agents Moe Smith and Izzy Einstein raided this restaurant in 1923. They dressed as fishermen and hired boats "with all the requisites." Those requisites called for an arrest under the Volstead Act. (RF.)

Mark's Restaurant was located at the south end of Woodcleft Avenue. It was later known as the Ship's Inn and now the Schooner. In the 1920s and 1930s, it was a famous speakeasy and favorite docking space for rum-running boats. Mark charged $1 per case to unload at his dock. Waiting trucks would speed the illegal cargo into New York City, where it would fetch top dollar.

The Sea Breeze Restaurant, a hotel and fishing station, was located at the south end of Miller Avenue at Richmond Avenue on Little Swift Creek. It was a rumrunner's meeting place and was raided by federal agents Moe Smith and Izzy Einstein in 1923. In 1933, other agents, who bought liquor, arrested bartender John Werzinger and left a summons for owner Herman Marschner. A later owner was Otto Kunz.

Ellison's Ferry Dock and Restaurant was located at the south end of Woodcleft Avenue. Ferries departed here for Point Lookout and High Hill Beach. Both Capt. Joe Raynor and the *Caliban* left from here and took out party boats for local organizations, such as B'Nai Israel. During Prohibition, Louis Joseph of the Bronx was arrested at the dock with 16 cases of liquor in his automobile.

The Prospect Gun Club was located on Meadow Island on Long Creek near Jones Inlet and was founded in 1881 by a group of New York sportsmen. Capt. Abe Smith sailed wealthy members to and from the property on the *Marguerite*. It was dubbed "Millionaires Row" because each member was worth at least a million dollars. A mighty nor'easter in 1918 took the building into the bay, and very little was recovered.

The only place that Freeporters could go for a dip in the ocean at the turn of the 20th century was Point Lookout. The *Sea Gull*, a two decker, chugged off from the foot of Woodcleft Avenue. On hot days, it carried so many passengers that it could not handle the returnees. They had to get back to Freeport by private boat at 50¢ a head.

Nassau-by-the-Sea was a summer bungalow colony located at Point Lookout Beach. The colony included a hotel and a number of bungalows owned by residents of Brooklyn, Manhattan, Freeport, and other places. The Ellison family owned a pavilion where people came to dance. The sail from Freeport took about 1.5 hours. A fire in 1918 destroyed about 25 structures.

The Norwood Hotel was also known as the Anchorage. It was built by John J. Randall at the north end of Randall Bay in 1908. It featured lodging, a barroom, billiard room, and dining room. Boats would take guests to Nassau-by-the-Sea, or they could bathe in the beach at the hotel. It later became known as the Casino. The wooden structure burned down in 1929.

The Casino was located on Casino Avenue and featured hotel rooms, a dining room, a pool, and a sandy beach. It was formerly known as the Anchorage. Leo Carrillo was the manager for one season. Many of the visiting actors to the LIGHTS Club stayed here. In 1920, federal agents arrested manager Dominick Ferrarra when they raided the club and found several cases of illegal liquor.

Freeport Bathing Beach was originally part of the Woodcleft Inn complex and was located at the north end of Woodcleft Canal. This waterfront pavilion had changing rooms, bathing suits for rent, and an out-of-tune piano that guests could play. Leo Carrillo, a member of the actors' colony, was a patron; he gave swimming lessons and held water contests.

RANDALL'S CHANNEL, FREEPORT, LONG ISLAND, N.Y.

Randall Bay is also known as Randall's Channel, with its northern terminus at the Casino and running south to Little Swift Creek and Baldwin Bay. The South Shore Yacht Club can be seen on the western shore. Houses line the eastern shore, which faces Roosevelt Avenue and South Long Beach Avenue. Many of those homes are built on pilings. Steam launches and sailboats dot the waterway.

In the early 1870s, surfmen were organized into companies of six or seven men as life savers who occupied government houses. They were on duty night and day from the middle of November until March 1. The station at Point Lookout was a half-mile west of Jones Inlet. It recruited its men, including Andrew Rhodes and Tip Smith, principally from Freeport and Baldwin.

The Meadow Island monument is located near the Loop Parkway to Point Lookout. It was once the site of the New Inlet Hotel and is a memorial to Charles Smith, who was killed by lightning inside the hotel in 1863. His sister Mary Elizabeth married Andrew Scott, and their son Charles lost his life on the battleship *Maine* when it was blown up in Havana Harbor on February 15, 1898.

Three

ACTORS' COLONY

The Long Island Good Hearted Thespian Society (LIGHTS) Clubhouse opened in 1916, located on Fairview Place and Branch Avenue. The building was 110 feet by 54 feet and featured porches that were 14 feet wide. The lighthouse rose to a height of 66 feet. It was powered by a high-intensity electric light. The club was open to anyone involved in theatrical pursuits. Among the 543 charter members were the stars of the day, many of whom summered in Freeport.

This is one of the three bars located in the lighthouse tower. This bar and the one located halfway up the tower required a jacket and tie. Some of the members objected and locked themselves in the barn for a week to emerge with a "wonderful hangover." As a result, a bar was established in the basement and became known as the "Pigs Club" where patrons could dress as they pleased.

The billiard room was one of the features of the club. It also boasted a dining room and kitchen with a celebrated chef, a gymnasium, and practice rooms. The club was only open during the summer, which was when theaters were closed. The actors celebrated every holiday, including Christmas, New Year's, and Valentine's Day. For Christmas, an actor played Santa Claus. One July, he arrived in a sleigh on streets covered with make-believe snow.

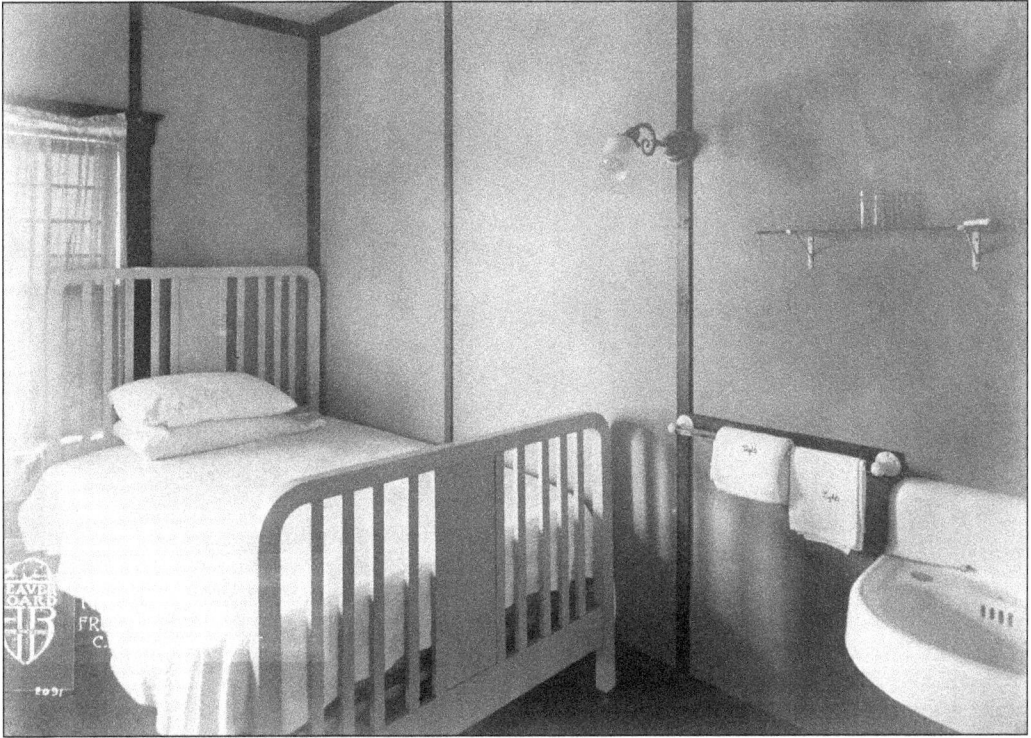

Bedrooms were located on the second floor; they were endowed and furnished by actor members. A plaque on the door indicated the donor. The stage was encircled by a balcony where the bedrooms were located. On the stage, actors practiced their routines and entertained three times a week, gratis. Shows did not start until 11:00 in the evening.

A group of actors pose inside the LIGHTS Club next to a sign advertising their Monster Vaudeville on Thursday, August 19, at the American Theatre. Among those in the picture are Harry Bulger, Victor Moore, William B. Hodge, Frank O'Brien, Frank Tinney, M.E. Manwaring, Bert Leighton, Bert Kalmar, Max Hart, Frank Harcourt, Frank Kaufman, Leo Carrillo, Arthur Deagon, and Frank Leighton.

The LIGHTS Club baseball team was composed of the following people: 1. Frank Kaufman, 2. Roy Cummings, 3. Willie O'Keefe, 4. Charlie ?, 5. unidentified, 6. George White, Norman Manwaring (booking agent), 8. Lou Kelly, 9. Jimmy Duffy, 10. unidentified, 11. Eddie Flanagan, 12. Benny Pierpont (booking agent), 13. unidentified, 14. the son of Eddie Flanagan, 15. Eddie O'Brien, and 16. Charles Cartmell.

The aerial view shows the field that was used for baseball games, Wild West shows, circuses, and polo matches, located north of the clubhouse. The polo team members included Vernon Castle, Leo Carrillo, Fred Stone, Will Rogers, and Frank Tinney. Elinor Smith and the Heinrich brothers would occasionally land their planes on the field. The beach was also popular with the members.

The actors had a chance to relax and have fun when they were at the club. In the 1910s and 1920s, the standard summer dress consisted of white flannels, pongee shirts, blue blazers, ties, and straw katies. However, on their own property, members wore the worst clothes imaginable. Old shirts and trousers were the order of the day as the actors enjoyed unusual pastimes.

Victor Moore (1876–1962) and Emma Littlefield (1883–1934) had a popular vaudeville act. Moore performed on Broadway in the role of Vice President Throttlebottom in *Of Thee I Sing* and also appeared in many movies. They came to Freeport in 1910 but eventually moved to Baldwin. Moore returned to Freeport and lived on South Long Beach Avenue. He was a charter member of the LIGHTS Club and was its first angel, or president.

Leo Carrillo (1881–1961) lived on Miller Avenue and then built a house—with a zoo—on West Lena Avenue, now Wilson Place. He began in vaudeville, telling dialect stories and graduated to Broadway and then the movies. Early in his career, he shared a dressing room with Will Rogers. On television, he played Pancho in the *Cisco Kid*. He was a charter member of LIGHTS and participated in all its activities.

Fred Stone (1873–1959) was one of the most important actors in Freeport. Although he summered in Amityville from 1915 on, he bought a house and erected a building for his father, L.P. Stone, in Freeport. He starred in vaudeville, musical comedy, and the movies. He was one of the founders of the LIGHTS Club and was involved in its circuses, cruises, and polo team. He also sponsored trophies for the Freeport Gun Club. (University of Washington Libraries, Special Collections, UW29826z.)

Lillian Russell (1861–1922) was an actress, singer, and star of the Weber and Fields Music Hall, where John Stromberg was the musical director. A section of Freeport was named after her, as were two streets. In 1902, Russell and her chauffeur were ticketed in Freeport for exceeding the eight-miles-per-hour speed limit. She referred to the local officials as "pig-headed ignoramuses." (LC.)

John Stromberg (1853–1902) was one of the first persons connected with the theater to come to Freeport in 1900. His estate was on Grand Avenue. He was a composer of popular music and was the musical director for Weber and Fields. His last song, "Come Down, Ma Evenin' Star," was sung by Lillian Russell after Stromberg committed suicide. He was a member of Wide Awake Fire Company. The Stromberg Park development was named after him. (DL.)

Ernest Ball (1878–1927) was a songwriter and an entertainer in vaudeville with his wife, Maude Lambert. Some of his songs include "When Irish Eyes Are Smiling," "Let the Rest of the World Go By," and "Will You Love Me in December as You Do in May." His life story was told in the film *Irish Eyes Are Smiling*. He was a charter member of the LIGHTS Club. (University of Washington Libraries Special Collections, UW29857z.)

Al Von Tilzer (1878–1956) of 255 Southside Avenue and his brother Harry (1872–1946) of South Bayview Avenue were songwriters, publishers, and performers. Al wrote the music for "Take Me Out to the Ball Game," and one of Harry's many songs is "Wait 'Till the Sunshines, Nellie." He and Harry were both charter members of the LIGHTS Club and active in their shows and benefits. (University of Washington Libraries, Special Collections, UW29824z.)

William W. Watson (c. 1880–1940), also known as "Sliding Billy," was a Dutch comedian known for his funny little slide. One of his shows in 1908 was *The Girls from Happyland*, which included Fanny Brice. His home was on Elm Place. His estranged wife, Nellie, was murdered in the 300 Club by a disgruntled waiter, a scandal in Freeport. He was a charter member of the LIGHTS Club. (University of Washington Libraries Special Collections, UW29823z.)

Gertrude Hoffmann (1886–1966) was renowned in vaudeville and on Broadway as a dancer, choreographer, and impersonator. In 1909, she was arrested in New York City at Hammerstein's Roof Garden above the Victoria Theater for her Salome dance, which was considered "indecent, suggestive, and immoral." Her summer home was at 463 South Bayview Avenue, and her husband, Max, was a charter member of the LIGHTS Club. (LC.)

Helene Hamilton and Jack Barnes (d. 1929) lived on Elm Street. As a vaudeville team, they traveled all over the world, including New Zealand and Australia. He also was a character actor in such productions as *Bobby Burnit* and *Dawn of a Tomorrow*. He was a charter member of the LIGHTS Club, and they participated in a benefit for Our Holy Redeemer Catholic Church and were in a number of LIGHTS productions.

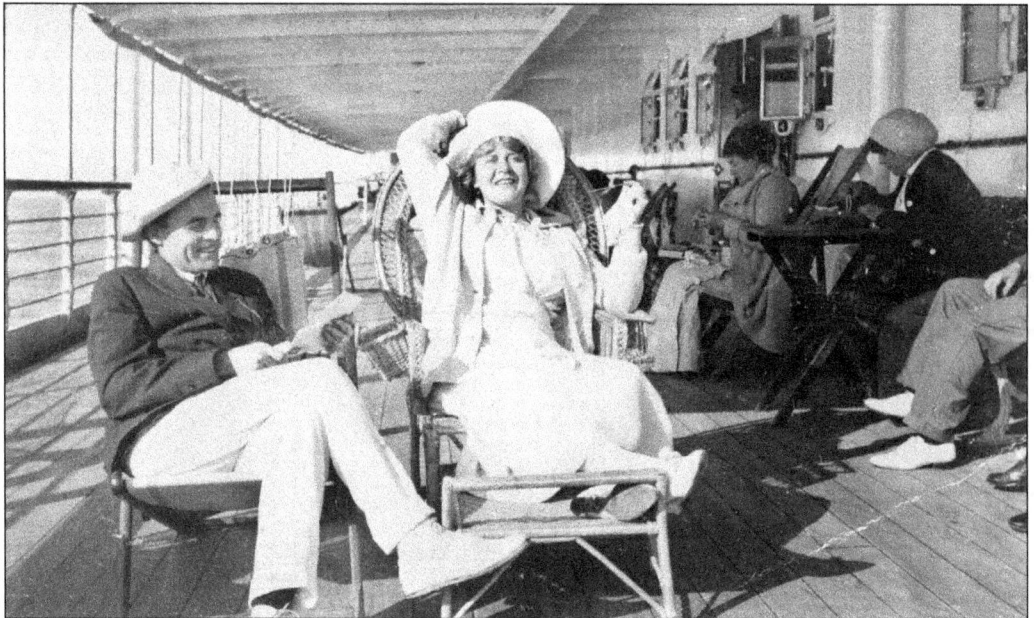

Arthur McWatters and Grace Tyson (1881–1942) performed in vaudeville in a song-and-dance act. They toured with McIntyre and Heath's Comedians. They settled in Freeport in 1916 and lived on Rose Street for 25 years. He was a charter member of the LIGHTS Club. They did a number of benefits for the synagogue and other organizations.

Ben Welch (c. 1877–1926), who lived on Nassau Avenue, was billed as a "cheerful Jewish comic" who performed song and dance in vaudeville and on Broadway. He was one of the 1908 pioneers who came to the actor's cottage colony in south Freeport. He spread the word of Freeport as a summer residence and that it would "be the Mount Olympus of the theatrical gods." (University of Washington Libraries Special Collections, UW29822z.)

Frank Tinney (1878–1940), pictured with his son Frank Jr., was called "the greatest natural comic ever developed in America." A vaudeville and Broadway comedian, his summer home was on South Long Beach Avenue. He appeared in the Ziegfeld Follies and the movie *The Governor's Boss*, filmed in Freeport. He was a charter member of the LIGHTS Club and played on its polo team.

39

The Amoros Sisters were billed as "those French girls." Heloise (right) and Josephine (left) were members of a family of acrobats, who performed in European circuses. They did juggling, trapeze work, sang, and danced. Heloise later did an act with her husband, George Obey. Josephine was married to Tony Wilson, who was also in trapeze work. Josephine opened a dance studio on Railroad Avenue. Obey later opened the Bayview Hardware store.

Ben Mulvey with Charlotte Amoros did an act together where they offered songs and acrobatic dances in a musical skit "A Night in Paris." They gave up the stage, and Ben started a painting and interior decorating business. He was a charter member of the LIGHTS Club and did many benefits for Our Holy Redeemer and B'Nai Israel. He was also a member of Hose No. 3.

The Four Ellsworths, from top to
bottom, were Harry, Una, Grace, and
John Marion, who played as a family for
many years. Harry also did a turn with
dancing girls, and Marion and Grace had
a song-and-dance act that was billed as
"the most clever children on the stage
today." The Ellsworths performed in
vaudeville and on Broadway. As charter
LIGHTS members, they did many benefits,
including one for the police department.

The vaudeville team of Coakley, Hanvey,
and Dunlevy, shown from top to bottom,
was a blackface feature act that sang,
danced, and talked. Mike Coakley lived
at 65 Nassau Avenue. Eileen Coakley, his
wife, often appeared with him. Lou Hanvey
had a ringing tenor voice and lived on Pine
Street until he moved to Baldwin. Coakley
did a number of benefits for Our Holy
Redeemer Roman Catholic Church. All
were charter members of the LIGHTS Club.

41

Reine Davies (1882–1938) was a sister of Marion Davies. She was known as the "Great American Beauty" and appeared in vaudeville, on Broadway, and in a few movies. The song associated with her is "Meet Me Tonight in Dreamland." She summered in a bungalow on Wilson Place in 1922. Davies threw a lawn party during which her neighbor Oscar Hirsch was shot by his wife, Hazel, on her property. (LC.)

Sophie Tucker (1887–1966) lived on Roosevelt Avenue and at 65 Nassau Avenue with her bandleader husband, Frank Westphal, who was a charter member of the LIGHTS Club. She was known as "the Last of the Red Hot Mamas," and her signature song was "Some of These Days." She opened Sophie Tucker's Garage on Merrick Road to keep her husband from spending all of his time at the LIGHTS Club. (University of Washington Libraries, Special Collections, UW29825z.)

Will Rogers (1879–1935) played the vaudeville circuit doing roping tricks. He was best known as a humorist and social commentator. Although he did not live in Freeport, he was a charter member of the LIGHTS Club and best friends with Fred Stone. He played on the Freeport polo team and demonstrated his riding and roping abilities at the Wild West Shows and cruises. (LC.)

Charles Middleton (1874–1949) and Leora Spellmeyer (1890–1945) of Roosevelt Avenue teamed up for a vaudeville act. He appeared in almost 200 movies and many plays. One of his most famous roles was Ming the Merciless in the Flash Gordon series. He was a charter member of the LIGHTS Club and played on its polo team. This photograph was taken in Oceanside with one of Anthony Fedden's horses.

William "Billy" Murray (1877–1954) became famous as the "Denver Nightingale." His strong tenor voice and very clear enunciation were suited to the acoustic format and fell out of favor with the rise of the electric microphone. He was the Bing Crosby of his time. He was a charter member of the LIGHTS Club and played on its baseball team. He lived on Southside Avenue. (PD.)

Arthur Deagon (c. 1871–1927) lived in a succession of homes on Randall Avenue and Pennsylvania Avenue and was one of the first actors to live in Freeport. He was a star in the Ziegfeld Follies. When rehearsing for George M. Cohan's *Merry Malones*, he died of a heart attack. He was a charter member of the LIGHTS Club and participated in many of its benefits, including one for the police department.

Four

SCHOOLS AND
RELIGIOUS INSTITUTIONS

Elizabeth Southard taught at a private school for children 10 years of age and younger during the Civil War in this building, which stood on the east side of South Main Street, across from the entrance to Smith Street and Bedell Street. She taught the primary subjects to about 20 or 25 students for a year or two, then married and closed the school.

About 1870, Presbyterian minister Rev. Marcus Burr organized the private Freeport Academy, located in the second floor of the building on the north side of Little Pine Street between Church Street and Main Street. It attracted students from Freeport and surrounding communities and existed for about 15 to 20 years. It was instituted because the district school gave only a rudimentary education.

The first Raynortown Schoolhouse, built in 1838, was located in the triangle where Main Street and Church Street intersect. It was a one-room building, dimly lit through small windows. A cast-iron box stove that burned wood was in the center of the room. The furniture consisted of stationary desks made of pine boards fastened to the sides of the room.

A second school replaced the original building in 1852. This one-story building was located on the west side of Main Street, north of Merrick Road. In 1857, a second floor was added to accommodate 200 scholars from ages four to 21. While carpenters were adding to the school, Andy Rhodes's wagon shop was rented for three months.

The first Grove Street School was a wooden building that opened in 1875. It was located on the northwest corner of Pine Street and Grove Street and was enlarged in 1882. On January 10, 1893, the wooden building burned down in a spectacular fire, which people tried to put out by throwing snowballs. This alerted the community of a need for a water department, fire hydrants, and an organized fire department.

In 1894, the second Grove Street School was built on the southeast corner of Grove Street and Pine Street at the cost of $30,000. This new, brick, 10-room high school was outfitted with up-to-the-minute requirements of the times. In 1903–1904, a large 10-room extension was added. The high school had well-equipped chemical and physical laboratories and manual and physical training departments.

Public School No. 2, Seaman Avenue, Freeport, L. I.

Because of overcrowding, the Seaman Avenue School was built in 1907 on the southwest corner of Seaman Avenue and Ocean Avenue to service northern Freeport. It had 10 rooms and an assembly room and accommodated 350 students. It was also called School No. 2 or the Washington School. It is now the district's administration building.

Further crowding and a need to service the southern section of Freeport led to the building of the Archer Street School in 1909. Also known as School No. 3 or the Lincoln School, the board of education used the same architect and plans that were used for the Seaman Avenue School to save money. Pictured is the kindergarten room with a fireplace. The students are dressed in costumes.

Freeport High School students held a strike in 1912 to protest the dismissal of a popular principal, Prof. Roy Leon Smith, by board of education president Samuel R. Smith. When the students arrived in the morning and heard the news, the boys immediately left the building to protest the action. The girls followed later.

High school students protested on Railroad Avenue around 1920 about conditions in the Grove Street School that were inadequate and out of date. The kindergarten-through-12th-grade school was so overcrowded that classes were held in the attic and basement. In the background is the honor roll of all Freeporters who served in World War I.

In 1922, village president Hilbert R. Johnson delivered the address at the laying of the cornerstone of the new Freeport High School. Officials from the village and the board of education were in attendance. The high school was built on the site of the Freeport cemetery, which was condemned. Most of the bodies of early settlers and Mexican and Civil War veterans were moved to Greenfield Cemetery.

The new Freeport High School opened in 1924 on the south side of Pine Street on the site of the old Freeport Cemetery. The school featured a gymnasium and an auditorium, as well as up-to-date science laboratories, home economics rooms, industrial arts facilities, and a library. As Freeport's population increased, the building was replaced by a new high school on Brookside Avenue in 1960.

Freeport elementary school students gathered around the Christmas tree in the original wooden Grove Street School. A calendar on the tree indicates that it was Christmas 1892, about three weeks before the building burned down. The blonde boy in the second row on the right is Elliott Ross, son of Lewis Ross, a prominent Freeporter.

The Freeport High School 1906 football team gathered around the Parrott rifle on the lawn of the school. Included in the picture are Steve Story, Fred Hunt, Owen Humphrey, Frank Pitcher, Vernon Colyer, Bob Miles, Roy Leon Smith (principal), Herb Tredwell, Milton Raynor, Harold Cook, and James Stiles. The Parrott rifle came from the USS *Hartford*, flagship of Adm. David Farragut during the Battle of Mobile Bay in 1864.

In 1833, under William B. Raynor, the Methodists bought a small wooden store on the west side of the Hempstead Babylon Turnpike, south of Seaman Avenue, and moved it to the John B. Powell farm at the corner of old Crooked Land and the Hempstead and Babylon Turnpike. The Sand Hole Church, which was in use for 25 years, was presided over by local and itinerant preachers.

A large piece of land was purchased on Pine Street, between Grove Street and Church Street, where the present United Methodist church is located. The first portion of the building was erected in 1891, followed by the newly constructed parsonage. Additions were made in 1915, and further improvements were made in 1928. The original facade was stucco, and the building had a tall steeple, which was lowered after it was hit by lightning.

The First Presbyterian Church was completed on May 13, 1860, at a cost of $5,255. The chapel, a gift of Susan Bergen in memory of her mother, Elizabeth Carman, was built about 1879. The manse was built in 1899. The Presbyterians remained in this building until 1964 when they sold it to the Salvation Army and built a larger church on South Ocean Avenue.

The Dean Street Chapel was the home of the Plymouth Brethren, "a Testament-based organization" founded in 1880 by the Reverend Charles Boynton, former minister of the First Presbyterian Church. At first, church members met at his home on North Main Street. As the congregation grew, there was a need for a permanent home, and the chapel, located at 23 West Dean Street, was built in 1923.

The Episcopal Church of the Transfiguration held its first services in 1892 at Raynor's Hall on Merrick Road as a mission church of the Cathedral of the Incarnation, Garden City. A lot was purchased at South Long Beach Avenue and Pine Street in 1893, and the church building was erected the next year. It was dedicated in September 1894. It was replaced by a larger building in 1951.

The Baptists first held services in 1890 and were incorporated on May 23, 1895. Their regular services were held in Raynor's Hall on Merrick Road until they constructed a chapel on Grove Street north of Merrick Road in 1904. It was a Shingle-style structure with Gothic windows and Grecian doors. William G. Miller was the architect and builder.

First Baptist Church of Freeport, N.Y.

e. o. nielsen

The original chapel of the First Baptist Church outgrew its usefulness. Land on the southwest corner of Long Beach Avenue and Pine Street was purchased, and ground was broken for a new church on March 23, 1927. The large fieldstone edifice was finished in 1928, and a parish house was added to the building.

The first mass for Roman Catholics in Freeport was held at the home of William Dougherty on Christmas Day around 1895 and was a mission of St. Agnes Parish in Rockville Centre. The first church on Pine Street and Grove Street was completed in 1900. It was a small wooden structure, and there were 10 or 12 shelters to house horses and carriages used by parishioners attending mass.

The first portion of the present-day Our Holy Redeemer Roman Catholic Church on Ocean Avenue and Pine Street opened on Easter Sunday 1911. It was designed by the firm of Lee and Hewitt in the Romanesque style and was built by Irish immigrant bricklayers. The church, including the massive bell tower, cost $80,000 to build.

The Bethel African Methodist Episcopal Church was founded in 1902 and built its first church around 1908 on Henry Street, just south of the railroad. About 1924, the congregants moved the building to Helen Avenue near Waverly Place. When the area became an urban renewal site in 1974, the congregation built a new church on North Main Street.

The Christ Lutheran Church was organized in 1909 and rented, for $5 a month, a portable chapel from the Church Extension Society, which was placed on the east side of North Main Street. As the congregation grew, it bought the Meadon Estate on the southwest corner of Grove Street and Randall Avenue and moved the chapel there.

Work on the new building for the Christ Lutheran Church began in 1925 during the pastorate of the Reverend Carl H. Miller. The property was 125 feet on Randall Avenue and 170 feet on North Grove Street. The building committee voted that the edifice be either of stone or brick, and on April 25, 1926, the new stone structure was dedicated. A chapel was added later.

Congregation B'Nai Israel met in 1915 at members' homes. Five years later, the first temple was built in northeast Freeport at Broadway and Mount Avenue. It remained at this location for 38 years and then sold its building to members of the Greek Orthodox faith. The building is now the home of the Refuge Apostolic Church. B'Nai Israel built a new center on North Bayview Avenue.

Glick Photo: Used by permission
Gathering for a Ring Meeting
Commodious Tabernacle in background
The Long Island Holiness Camp Meeting
106 Prince Avenue, Freeport, L. I.

Beginning in 1919, the Long Island Holiness Camp Meeting, also known as Camp Roosevelt, made Freeport its headquarters and held annual 12-day sessions at its location at Prince Avenue and North Long Beach Avenue. Services were held at the large auditorium on the grounds. The property also contained a dining hall, office building, preacher's cabin, dormitory, recreational center, and caretaker's cottage.

The first worshippers of the First Church of Christ Scientist of Freeport met in the Levy Building in 1920. Their building on Merrick Road was the Christian Science Building in the 1939 New York World's Fair. It was moved in six sections. They added an elliptically shaped auditorium with a balcony. Surrounding the cornerstone are four bricks from the chimney of Mary Baker Eddy.

The Bennington Park Baptist Church began as a mission that met in Rev. William Jones's home. Within months, the congregants moved to 154 East Merrick Road to organize the mission into a church. It was named the Greater Second Baptist Church and was incorporated in 1931. Members bought a small church building at 129 East Merrick Road in 1933. Since then, a large church has been built on this site.

Bennington Park Church of God was located at 10 Helen Avenue in Freeport in the late 1930s. The first minister was William Hull. The programs offered by the church included Sunday school and a choir. Some members included Lysia Marsh, Elyse Hull, Herman Parrish, Benjamin Simmons, Larry Ross, and Leon Deas. The church's new building is located on the corner of Grand Avenue and Lakeview Avenue.

Five

HOMES

Woodbine, located now on West Woodbine Avenue, was built around 1890 by John J. Randall. It was one of the most spectacular houses in Freeport. The Queen Anne Victorian features a Byzantine dome, fish-scale siding, scrolled plaster ceilings, and oak parquet floors. The original house was divided by John J. Randall. According to his grandson, the house was too big for one family. The eastern half of the house was used as a rooming house and eventually burned down. (CK.)

"Stonehurst" located at 314 South Ocean Avenue was built by architect Benjamin Homan. This Shingle-style home, with fieldstone accents and a magnificent chimney, included several outer buildings on 1.5 acres of property. In 1913, Max Grifenhagen purchased the house as a summer residence. He was the noted sheriff of New York County, an alderman, and a city registrar. His wife, Carrie, lived here until her death in 1942.

A small bayman's cottage from the Civil War era was the home of Dr. and Mrs. Horace T. Evans for 50 years. Dr. Evans was a noted professor of anatomy at New York Medical College. His wife, Gertrude, an Egyptologist, was renowned for her art and photography. They made many additions to the house, which is now the nine-room, four-level home of the Freeport Historical Society.

This two-story home of J. Huyler Ellison at 41 Wallace Street featured world-renowned gardens. In addition to a spectacular Japanese garden, the grounds included plantings of irises, peonies, phlox, and roses. In 1910, Pres. Theodore Roosevelt dined at this home after he attended the Southern New York State Volunteer Firemen's Association Convention. Jennie (1880–1978) and Charles Reitmeyer (1874–1933) of the Plaza Theater were the next owners.

On the corner of Main Street and Southside Avenue stands the house of John C. Raynor. It dates back to the Civil War. He was in the oyster business as a planter and dealer. The two-story farmhouse has a wraparound porch on the east and south sides. It was said that black crepe was draped around the flagpole as an emblem of sorrow for the death of Abraham Lincoln.

The home of Samuel R. Smith at 135 Smith Street occupied the entire block from Ocean Avenue to Grove Street. His Shingle-style home featured a turret in the Romanesque style. A 1907 Locomobile is parked in front of the house with Roy G. Greenleaf in the front passenger seat and Wally Smith at the wheel. In the backseat is Rev. Charles Boynton.

Frank and Lena Willetts lived on Lena Avenue. Frank was in construction in the Bronx, and Lena was the daughter of John J. Randall. They were married in 1906 at Woodbine and had two children, Elizabeth and John. The couple ran the John J. Randall Company. This house, built on the Woodbine property, features a green tile roof and huge columns in the Colonial Revival style.

The Pitman Combs home on South Bayview Avenue was built in 1893. The first floor of this farmhouse features a large living room with a music alcove and a bedroom. Combs had a door from his dining room that led to his grocery store where he cashed checks, delivered messages, and acted as sort of a bank. In 1912, Combs opened a new market on Atlantic Avenue and Bayview Avenue.

The home at 211 Grand Avenue is a center hall Colonial, built around 1860. The distinctive Italianate porch was added to the home in the 1880s. It was the homestead of a large farm, which covered most of what is now northeast Freeport. This was home to the Southard family, who named it Hillcrest, except for a brief period in the 1920s when it became the property of the Ku Klux Klan.

The first home of William G. and Mary Randall Miller, located on Ocean Avenue, was three stories high and boasted ornate gingerbread, a decorated roof and tower, and sleeping porches. The family later moved to a smaller 27-room house at 157 South Ocean Avenue. The move was prompted when one of their sons died and the rest of their children married or went away to school. (FML.)

One of William G. Miller's many homes in Freeport was located at 137 South Ocean Avenue. He downsized from his previous home to this 27-room house as his children grew up and left home. One of its unique features was a grass tennis court. Shaded porches graced the front of the home, and a widow's walk topped the roof.

Built about 1908 by leading real estate developer Jacob Post (1874–1964), this Arts and Crafts–style house is located at 136 North Ocean Avenue. When constructed, the house featured a double-faced fireplace between the living room and a wraparound porch. The first floor had beamed ceilings and cherrywood paneling. Olive Boulevard, now Sunrise Highway, was named after Post's daughter. He was a builder and developer for many years.

At the turn of the 20th century, Lena Avenue ended at Long Beach Avenue. A real estate dispute between John J. Randall and the Warranty Realty Company developed over the placement of the roads. This led John J. Randall to erect a house "built in one day." It was framed and partially shingled within 24 hours and is referred to as the "spite house."

Stearns Park, Freeport, N. Y.

Hugo Stearns was a wealthy ostrich feather importer and merchant in Manhattan. Around 1905, he purchased a large tract of land north of the railroad along Pennsylvania Avenue and created Stearns Park, one of the finest and most exclusive residential parks on Long Island. His first home on the northeast corner of Pennsylvania Avenue and Prince Street was a sprawling Craftsman-style bungalow with low-pitched roofs.

FOR SALE

Sisters Myrtis Fish (d. 1928) and Dr. Mary Fish Fleckles (d. 1935) lived at 28 East Seaman Avenue. Myrtle was a lawyer who graduated from the New York School of Law, a probation officer, and the founder of a home for girls in Long Island City. Dr. Fleckles was one of Brooklyn's leading physicians. A graduate of the New York Medical College and Hospital for Women, she specialized in obstetrics and pediatrics. (MC.)

This Shingle-style house at 278 South Long Beach Avenue was the summer residence of Mrs. Frank T. McGlynn of Manhattan. It features a wraparound porch, interesting window details, and multiple peaked roofs. Mrs. McGlynn contributed to the building fund of Our Holy Redeemer Roman Catholic Church. Considered one of the social leaders in Freeport, the wedding of her daughter Catherine was "one of the most notable in Long Island society."

This spacious 1903 Shingle-style Victorian at 119 Miller Avenue features a front porch and tower typical of the period. It was the home of William P. Miller, president of the W.P. Manufacturing Company of Greenpoint and, later, the Long Island Traction Company. He was a charter member and vice commodore of the South Shore Yacht Club.

William Furst (1852–1917) lived at 239 South Ocean Avenue in this Shingle-style house with wraparound porches and a multiple-peaked roof. He was the musical director of the Empire Theater and associated with David Belasco. He wrote songs for productions in which Maud Adams, Geraldine Farrar, and Lillian Russell starred. He tripped over a flower pot at his home, injured his foot, and died of a cerebral embolism. (MC.)

Benjamin Homan was the architect of the pagoda on Randall Bay. It was the summer home of H. Lyon Smith, a Pennsylvania millionaire. Though there was no heating unit, the 12-room house did have an open fireplace. Smith could step off his back porch onto his boat. On the Fourth of July in 1913, he decorated the house with about 500 electric lights.

Ocean Avenue, Freeport, L. I.

Imported and Published by The Freeport News Co.

The brick Victorian at the left was built in 1898 by Owen Humphrey, a contractor and real estate developer. He also built the Grove Hotel, which can be seen in the background. A later occupant of the house was Freeport mayor Clinton Flint. In 1915, the empty lot was owned by David Levy. The other houses on Ocean Avenue were owned by Charles Hawkins, Mary Wells, and Lucy Wood.

T.C.B. "Tommy" Forbes lived in this Colonial, shingled home with palladium windows at 321 Archer Street. After his retirement from the automobile business, Tommy entered the real estate business in Freeport. Forbes Place was named after him. He also was a member of the Freeport Polo Club. Additionally, he was president of the Freeport Railroad Company that ran the "Fishermen's Delight" trolley to the Great South Bay Ferry Company, which he also owned.

Brooklyn businessman George W. Bergen (1814–1900) built a house on Merrick Road in 1869. It featured a 50-foot tower and many wings. The property included a flower garden, greenhouse, barns, carriage house, root cellar, poultry house, workshop, icehouse, stables, and a birdhouse designed to be a replica of the house. A beautiful five-acre park that stretched from Merrick Road to the railroad tracks was situated north of the house.

Seen from the roof of the home of Col. James Dean, the president of Freeport from 1902 to 1905, is the home of Lewis Ross (d. 1929) at 188 Archer Street. The Methodist church is in the background. Ross was a pioneer Freeport merchant and heavily involved in real estate. He was one of the original signers of the village incorporation papers.

For a short time, Ernest Randall (1871–1934) lived in this large house between Pearsall Avenue and Randall Avenue on North Long Beach Avenue. This shingle-sided home featured three levels of porches and massive columns. He was a prominent banker, architect, and real estate developer. He was the son of John J. Randall, brother of John J. Randall II and Lena Randall Willets. He was president of Freeport in 1914.

The home at 32 South Bergen Avenue is an example of a Shingle-style Victorian with porches, bay windows, and a porte cochere typical of the style. An earlier owner was William Grace, a real estate broker in Brooklyn, and his family. Records from 1910 indicate he employed a Swedish maid and a coachman who lived in the house. A later owner was Allan Cruickshank, whose father, John, was president of Freeport from 1926 to 1927.

The house of Victor Moore (1876–1962) on South Long Beach Avenue at Roosevelt Avenue is a 14-room Spanish villa with 178 feet of water frontage, marble floors in the living room, elaborate grillwork, and a three-bedroom guesthouse shaped like a lighthouse. It was built around 1927, and one of its early owners was Wilbur Johnson, a well-known advertising executive who was a commodore of the South Shore Yacht Club. Moore moved in around 1940.

Guy Lombardo (1902–1977), the famous orchestra leader of the Royal Canadians, and his wife, Lilliebell, lived in this modern home located at 710 South Grove Street. On the first floor were a 30-by-30-foot sunken living room, a large dining room, and kitchen. The master bedroom was the size of a suite. The Lombardo property had an in-ground swimming pool and a boat slip that ran under his house.

Six

PERSONALITIES

Caroline G. Atkinson (1866–1949) began her teaching career in the Freeport schools on August 30, 1885, in the four-room school on Pine Street and Grove Street. She taught all grade levels, and her former students said that she was the best teacher they ever had. After 52 years of service, Atkinson retired in 1937. She was a member of the First Baptist Church where she was elected an honorary deaconess.

Pictured are Bergen family members, from left to right, George W. Bergen (1814–1900), George P. (1849–1909), William Clinton Story (1892–1918), and daughter Elizabeth Story. George W. was a senior member of the Valentine, Bergen & Co., wholesale grocers of Brooklyn. He moved to Freeport permanently in 1869. George P. Bergen was his son and a principal in his father's grocery business. They were active members of the Presbyterian church.

Florence Carman, a society matron, is pictured in a carriage in front of her house at 118 West Merrick Road. She married Dr. Edwin Carman, a prominent physician. In 1914, she was accused of murdering Lulu Bailey, a patient of her husband. The first trial ended in a hung jury, and a young George Morton Levy defended her in the second trial. She was acquitted.

Merritt Cutler (1898–1987) was a student at Freeport High School and was selected to represent Freeport on the Bay View Tennis Club team in 1914. During World War I, he received the Distinguished Service Cross. He returned to Freeport after the war and studied art at Pratt School of Design. He became the commander of the William Clinton Story Post of the American Legion in 1919. He competed at Wimbledon in the 1920s.

Dr. John W. Dodd (c. 1894–1973) was the superintendent of the Freeport public schools from 1925 to 1961. In 1917, he was the principal of Columbus Avenue School. When World War I broke out, he enlisted. Later, he was appointed principal of Freeport High School and was eventually named superintendent. He supervised the addition to Archer Street School and was a member of the American Legion.

J. Huyler Ellison was involved in the steam and hot water-heating business. He devoted much of his time to the Freeport Fire Department and Vigilant Hose Company. In 1915, he was appointed private secretary to Congressman Frederick Hicks. He belonged to the Elks and the American Legion. A village trustee, he headed Playland Park in the late 1920s. He was a personal friend of Col. Theodore Roosevelt.

Stella Foreman (1878–1954) had real estate holdings throughout Long Island and was an astute businesswoman. She was a member of the Freeport Golf Club and the Ladies' Afternoon Euchre Club and sang at the Presbyterian Christmas exercises. She handled the land of Natta Stromberg Sigmond. She and her brother C. Milton Foreman (1875–1955) were the principal owners in the Freeport Development Company. She lived at 20 South Ocean Avenue.

William Foreman (1847–1896) came to
Freeport from Canada and joined the
lumber firm of Carman, Raynor & Co.
as a partner. When his partner died in
1891, he took sole control. Originally
located on the waterfront east of South
Main Street and Atlantic Avenue,
the firm moved to Commercial Street.
His son C. Milton Foreman owned
Foreman's hardware, two lumberyards,
and considerable residential property.

Chester Fulton (1871–1953), at
right, and his son Chester Curtis
(1898–1955) ran the Fulton Funeral
Home on Merrick Road. Chester
came to Freeport in 1904 and bought
Carman Peasell's funeral home.
He moved to his Merrick Road
location in 1914. Chester was active
in the community. He was a charter
member of the Elks, a member of
the Excelsior Hook and Ladder
Company, and the Exchange Club.

Mabel Pauline Guest served as a nurse during World War I. She enlisted for military service and, while waiting for overseas deployment, served in the Port Washington Red Cross Hospital during the Spanish flu epidemic. She died of the disease on October 30, 1918. At Freeport High School, she was part of a minstrel show to raise funds to build an auditorium in the village.

John N. Hartmann (d. 1939) was born in Philadelphia. At the age of 26, he joined the New York City Fire Department and retired in 1910 as a captain. For 10 years, he lectured on fire safety. He was chief of the Freeport Police Department from 1920 to 1939. He was hired at the time the Village of Freeport was reorganizing the police department. He had the reputation of maintaining tight control of the department.

Augustus Herring (1867–1926) was an American aviation pioneer involved in the glider experiments of Octave Chanute. He built and flew gliders of his own design. Herring also briefly worked for Samuel Langley, who was the principal competitor to the Wright brothers. In 1909, Herring created the Herring-Curtiss Company with Glenn Curtiss. He was married to Freeport-born Lillian Mellen and lived on South Main Street. (CA.)

Albin Johnson (1874–1933) was born in Sweden and attended Freeport High School and Brooklyn Law School. He joined his brother Hilbert in a law practice. He was the village police justice and a most universally beloved man. He was called the "Great Joiner;" it was said he belonged to more fraternal organizations than any other resident of Freeport. His memberships included the Elks, Exchange Club, American Legion, and the Odd Fellows.

Hilbert Johnson (1888–1953) was born in Freeport and graduated from Freeport High School and New York University Law School. He was a village trustee, president, counsel, and police judge. As the unofficial historian of the village, he wrote numerous articles for local papers and was the first president of the Freeport Historical Society in 1940. He was a member of the Elks, Exchange Club, and Hose Company No. 4.

George Morton Levy (1888–1977) was founder and president of the Roosevelt Raceway. In Freeport High School, he was on the baseball team and captain of the football team. He was a graduate of New York University and opened his law office in Freeport. He defended Florence Carman in her second murder trial. In the 1930s, he defended men accused of rum-running. He is pictured (left) with Dr. Edwin Carman. (LC.)

Guy Lombardo (1902–1977), standing, was the leader of the Royal Canadians band, famous for their New Year's Eve celebrations. In the 1930s, he built his home on Grove Street after visiting Otto's Sea Grill restaurant, owned by Otto Koglin, and seeing the property across Woodcleft Canal. Later, he opened Guy Lombardo's East Point House and ran the shows at the Jones Beach Marine Stadium. Some called him "Mr. Freeport" because of his involvement in the community.

Charles M. Manly (1876–1927) was an American engineer who assisted Samuel Langley in building the Great Aeodrome, a large manned airship. In 1900, he developed an improved engine, the Manly-Balzer engine. In 1903, he made two attempts to fly the machine. Both failed and he plunged into the Potomac River. He also worked with the Glenn Curtiss Aeroplane Company. His summer home was on Rose Street.

William G. Miller (1853–1931) and his wife, Mary Randall (c. 1851–1917), were prominent citizens of Freeport. She was John J. Randall's sister, and he was his business partner. Randall and Miller developed large tracts, building streets, erecting houses, and opening up canals. They also built hotels, pavilions, bathing accommodations, docks, and a trolley and ferry line. Miller was president of Freeport from 1893 to 1900 and served in the New York State Assembly.

Stephen P. Pettit (1880–1925) was president of the Citizens' National Bank on Merrick Road and a prominent player in the real estate market. He served three years as sheriff of Nassau County and initiated the development of the actors' colony. He was president of the Freeport Trotting Association and played polo against such players as Will Rogers, Vernon Castle, and Fred Stone. He also was an exalted ruler of the Freeport Elks.

David Pettigrew (d. 1934), known as "Smiling Dave," was a sergeant with the Freeport Police Department and died while making an arrest during a street brawl at the Moose Clubhouse. He emigrated from Scotland in 1904, and served in the US Navy patrolling the coast during World War I. He was the second Freeport police officer to die in the line of duty.

Irving "Honey" Potter played all over Long Island with his African American jazz band. During World War I, he was in the cornet section of the 367th Infantry band at Camp Upton. Called the "king pin" of all jazz outfits, his band provided entertainment for the Freeport Democratic Club, the Elks Club, the American Legion, and the 1922 Firemen's Association of the State of New York Golden Jubilee anniversary.

85

Originally from Brooklyn, John J. Randall (1846–1924) came to Freeport in 1885 and purchased large farms. Randall developed many residential sections and became known as "the Father of Freeport." He also dug several canals and erected homes and public buildings. He established the first bank in Freeport. Ultimately, he donated Randall Park to the village in his will. His magnificent home was known as Woodbine.

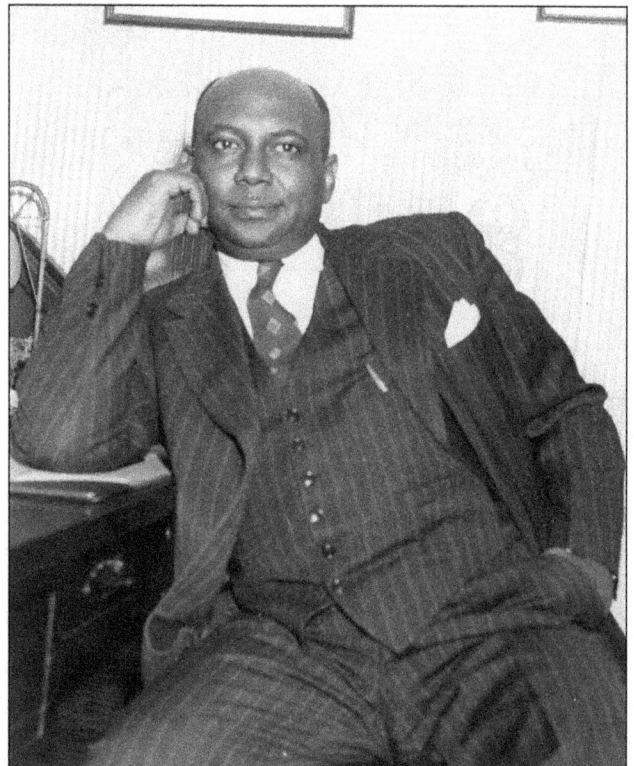

Moxey Rigby (1892–1962), a graduate of Freeport High School, was Nassau County's first African American judge. Upon graduation, Moxey was determined to become an attorney. As a waiter at the local Elks Club, he earned enough money to enroll in New York Law School and graduated in 1925. He was appointed to the Nassau District Attorney's Office in 1941. The Moxey Rigby apartments on Merrick Road are named in his honor.

Dr. Reginald Heber Scott (d. 1959) was the rector of the Transfiguration Episcopal Church from 1914 until he retired in 1957. He helped found the Freeport Memorial Library and served many years as a trustee and president of the board. He was also the chaplain for the Spartan Lodge of Masons and the Freeport Fire Department.

Charles Sigmond was a real estate agent who developed most of Russell Park. He also built the Sigmond Opera House on South Main Street. He married Natta Stromberg, the widow of John. Sigmond operated a hotel at Point Lookout and was a social manager at the Fountain Inn in Lynbrook. He was a charter member of the Elks and served for six years as a village of Freeport trustee.

Elinor Smith (1911–2010) grew up in Freeport. She was the daughter of the vaudevillian Tom Smith. She became fascinated with airplanes when she was six years old. Smith soloed at 15, earned her pilot's license the following year, and performed the daring stunt of flying under the four East River bridges at 17 years old. In the 1920s, her fellow pilots voted her the best female pilot in America.

Hiram Smith (1859–1925) was president of Freeport from 1906 to 1907. He also served as president of the Freeport Board of Education, president of the public library, supervisor of the town of Hempstead, and chief of the Freeport Fire Department. Additionally, he was a member of the Hempstead Bay Yacht Club and founding member of the Milburn Country Club. He also was an honorary member of the D.B.P. Mott Post of the Grand Army of the Republic (GAR).

Samuel R. Smith (1862–1931) organized the Bank of Far Rockaway in 1888 and was president of the Bank of Long Island. His wife, Ella, was the daughter of Rev. Charles Boynton. Smith was one of the guiding influences in the incorporation of the village of Freeport. Additionally, he served 12 years on the school board, eight as president. He was also active in the Methodist church.

William Clinton Story (1892–1918) was a 1908 graduate of Freeport High School, where he was salutatorian. He graduated from Princeton in 1913 with honors. When the United States entered World War I, he enlisted with the hopes of becoming an aviator. He died near Memphis, Tennessee, during a training flight. The William Clinton Story American Legion Post was named in his honor.

Archer B. Wallace (1876–1931) was the son of George Wallace and served in Company K, 71st Regiment during the Spanish-American War. As police justice, he adjudicated Lillian Russell's speeding case. Wallace's first loves were the Freeport Fire Department (Ever Ready Hose Company) and the Freeport Elks. He held many positions in both organizations and traveled extensively on their behalf. (VOF.)

George Wallace (c. 1849–1918) was a lawyer, president of Freeport from 1900 to 1902, a state assemblyman, and the second nominator for Theodore Roosevelt for governor. In his law practice, Wallace handled a case attempting to abolish separate colored schools. He was also instrumental in the formation of Nassau County. Wallace bought the *South Side Observer* and ran the newspaper for years. He also had a large real estate business.

Seven

GOVERNMENT AND PUBLIC SERVICES

The Colonial Revival–style Freeport Post Office was constructed in 1933 on Merrick Road. The exterior is typical of the buildings erected by the postal service. What sets Freeport's apart are the two William Gropper murals done for the Treasury Relief Art Program (TRAP) New Deal program. "Suburban Post in Winter" and "Air Mail" are oil-on-canvas paintings and can be seen on the east and west walls. The building is in the National Register of Historic Places.

Excelsior Hook and Ladder Company No. 1 was formed in December 1874. The truck was housed in a shed in the back of Mead's bakery on the east side of Main Street south of Merrick Road. The company was named by its first captain, "Uncle Billy" Patterson. The firehouse was built in 1882 on the west side of Parsonage Avenue, later known as Church Street.

Wide Awake Engine Company No. 1 was formed in 1893 after a fire destroyed the Grove Street School. Originally, the company rented space in a livery stable on South Main Street. Permanent headquarters on Church Street south of Pine Street were established. The company moved to its third firehouse around 1924, when a new headquarters building was completed on North Main Street. Charles I. Baldwin was the first captain.

Ever Ready Hose Company No. 1 was organized in 1894. George Wallace was the first captain. The company leased property on Bedell Street and built a firehouse in 1895. In 1915, it moved to a new firehouse on Southside Avenue between South Main Street and Bedell Street. This land had been donated by Cadman Fredericks.

Under the direction of Rowland Mayland, Vigilant Hose Company No. 2 was organized in 1894 and was housed on North Main Street. Equipment included a hand-drawn hose reel. In 1919, the company moved to new quarters on North Main Street. A final move was made to the fire department's headquarters on North Main Street in almost the exact location where the first building stood. (MG.)

Bay View Hose Company No. 3 was created in 1895. At first, members met at the home of their captain, H. Asa Nichols. In 1899, their first firehouse was constructed on Atlantic Avenue. They moved into a new building on Bayview Avenue south of Atlantic Avenue in 1918. The area was known as Coe's Neck, so the company's first hose reel jumper was named the "Coe's Neck Stump Jumper."

Patriot Hose Company No. 4 came into existence in 1911 to protect the northwest quadrant of the village. Its firehouse was built in 1913 on the eastern end of the power house property, now on Sunrise Highway. The original building was moved to North Long Beach Avenue and is the present Exempt Firemen's Association Hall. The company moved into its new building in 1932. Hilbert Johnson was the first captain.

When the northeast section was annexed in 1923, the Russell Hose Company became part of the Freeport Fire Department. Originally, it was No. 2 of the Roosevelt Fire Department and became Russell Hose No. 5. This neighborhood was known as Russell Park and was named after actress Lillian Russell. The company's first firehouse was on Leonard Avenue in 1913, which was remodeled in 1929. Their first captain was William Pearsall.

The village board appointed John J. Dunbar as the first peace officer in 1892. The force used bicycles until the late 1930s, when the patrol car was introduced. At the turn of the 20th century, the typical complaint concerned wild horses, wandering sheep, or destructive cattle. Pictured on bicycles in front of village hall are Capt. Carl Darenburg (left) and Officer Anthony Fedden.

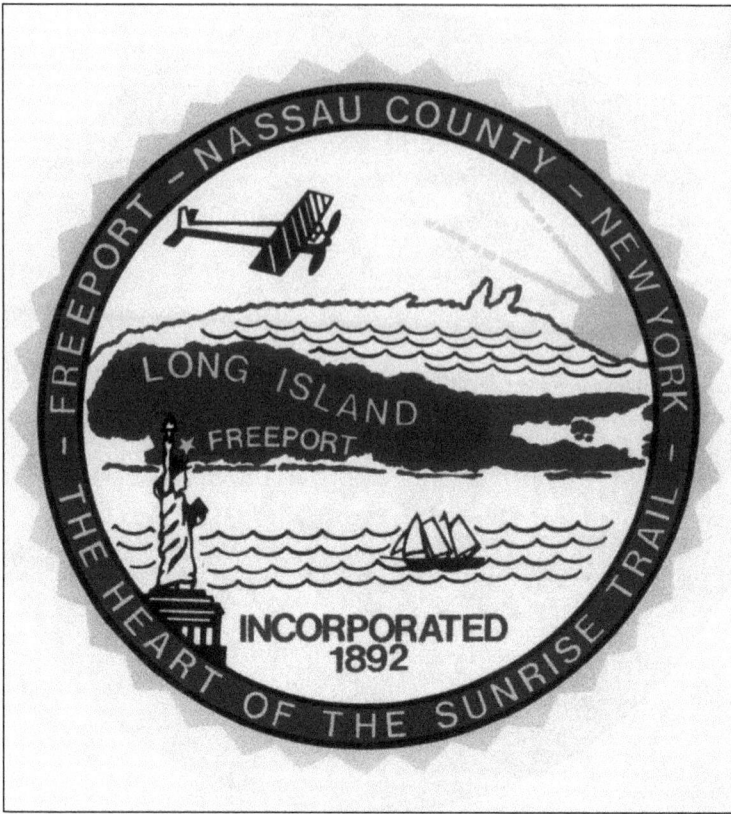

The village seal was designed by local artist Louis F. Fleming and was adopted in 1928 during the Clinton M. Flint administration. The seal includes the words, "Freeport–Nassau County–New York–The Heart of the Sunrise Trail–Incorporated 1892." A star indicates Freeport's location on Long Island. Freeport was one of the first villages on Long Island to adopt a seal.

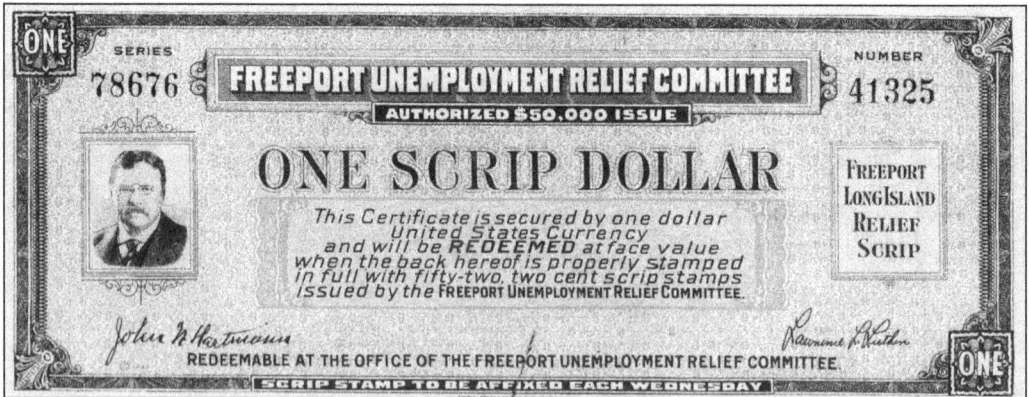

The Freeport Unemployment Relief Committee issued scrip in April 1933 to be used only in the village of Freeport. This issuance was intended to stimulate trade and provide funds to carry on the relief work of the committee. The scrip was the size of the original dollar bill. The denominations were either $1 or 25¢ and were issued against US currency.

On Memorial Day 1924, a library, designed by architect Charles M. Hart, was dedicated as the first war memorial library in New York State. In 1925, the Freeport Library officially changed its name to the Freeport Memorial Library. Three years later, a memorial tablet was dedicated. It bears the names of Freeporters who died while serving in the military during the Civil War, Spanish-American War, and World War I.

Established in 1884, the public library was located in the Freeport Schools for many years. In 1903, Freeport rejected Andrew Carnegie's offer to build a library in the village. It would be 23 years before Freeport would get a separate library building. Large windows, two fireplaces, and a soaring ceiling were architectural elements of the library's main reading room. The book stacks were located behind the door on the right. (FML.)

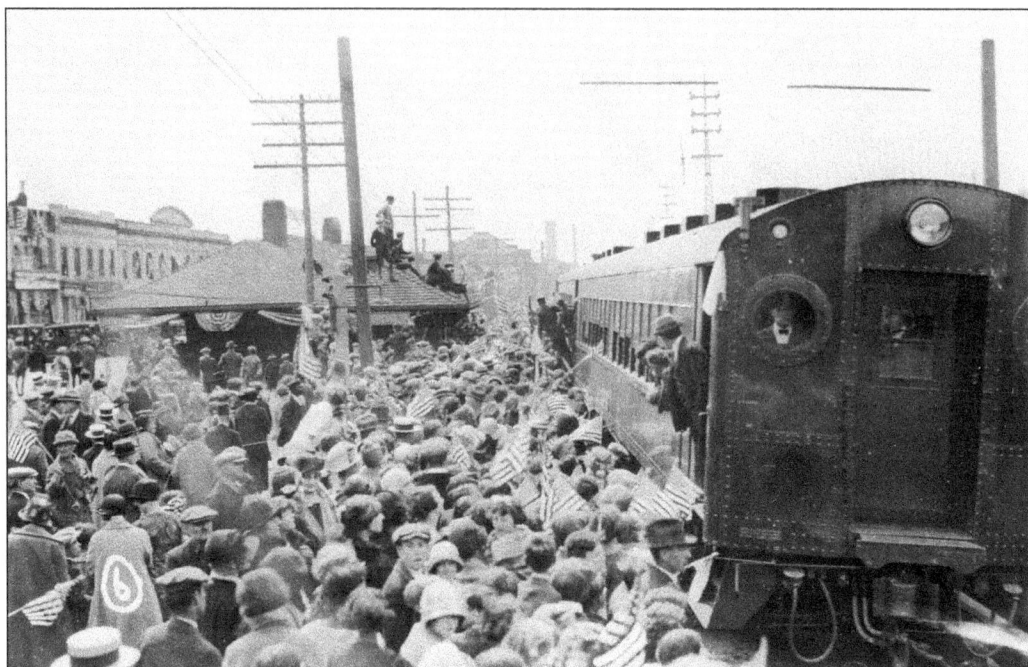

Freeport welcomed the first electric train in 1925. As the 14 railcars entered the station, five airplanes from Mitchel Field dropped clusters of lilacs. Along the route from New York City to Babylon, railroad stations were decorated with flags and bunting. Freeport celebrated with a parade of 2,000 marchers, bands, and fireworks. Freeporters crowded the platform and sat on the station roof to welcome the train.

Eight members of the Freeport Police Department championship pistol team around 1932–1933 are at the Freeport Pistol and Rifle Range, located just south of Freeport Municipal Stadium. The man in the middle of the second row is Peter Elar, and Chief John Hartmann is at the far right. The two men on the left in the first row are David Pettigrew (far left) and Ray Knipe. The range opened in 1931.

Pres. Clinton Flint, with the trowel, laid the cornerstone of village hall, located on North Ocean Avenue. The men to his right are trustee George Bird and village counsel Hilbert Johnson. The building includes offices, a courtroom, council chamber, meeting room, and police headquarters as well as vault equipment. The building is a replica of Independence Hall in Philadelphia. It opened in 1929.

The village of Freeport has its own courtroom located on the south end of village hall. When police justice Albin Johnson died in 1933, the family donated his picture, which is draped in black and hanging on the wall. From left to right are Robert E. Patterson, president; Hilbert Johnson, police justice and brother of Albin; and George Bird, trustee.

A Freeport village employee prepares the road in front of Ernest Randall's house on North Long Beach Avenue, just north of the railroad. Each spring, the department improved where necessary and oiled to allay the surface dust in the most traveled sections. Freeport road workers spread thousands of bushels of oyster and clamshells on village streets. In those days, men toiled nine hours for $1.50.

The need for a water system was evident when the school burned down in 1893. The original system had deep wells from which pure filtered water was pumped into the iron standpipe on the right. This tiny, brick pumping station was enlarged to include an electric plant that first went into operation in April 1898. It stood on what was then Centre Street, now Sunrise Highway.

Municipal plant No. 1 was expanded over the years by adding wings to the east and west and raising the roof. Eventually, the plant was powered by diesel engines. A water tower was added to maintain water pressure. Freeport is one of three communities on Long Island that generates its own electricity.

Located on the triangle of Main Street and Church Street, the cannon named Trubia was dedicated on July 4, 1902, by the Mott Post of the GAR. It was a Spanish gun that was 12,040 pounds, was made in 1874, and was captured at Morro Castle, Santiago, Cuba, in the Spanish-American War. The village worked with the Brooklyn Navy Yard to release this trophy gun to Freeport.

The Brooklyn Water Works (Milburn Pumping Station) was a three-story brick Romanesque Revival building, designed by Frank Freeman in 1888. It was one of a series of pumping stations along the south shore that provided water to the city of Brooklyn. After New York City turned to the Upstate for its water, the station was only used in an emergency. The oyster industry was adversely affected by Brooklyn's demand for water.

The municipal stadium was completed in 1931 and drew up to 10,000 fans for Midget Auto Races. A semiprofessional baseball team, the Penn Red Caps, played there, and the Brooklyn football Dodgers used it as their midweek training site. The stadium was constructed of reinforced concrete and originally had a capacity of 2,027. Other facilities included a football field, one-fifth of a cinder track, and a baseball field. Additionally, there were six tennis courts. (MH.)

Eight

RECREATION

Starting in 1913, the Freeport Railroad Company trolley ran from the Freeport Club down to Freeport Point to connect with the Great South Bay Ferry Company to Point Lookout. On the front seat are, from left to right, John J. Randall, William G. Miller, and Smith Cox. The man sitting by the second door is Stephen Pettit and behind him are George Morton Levy and Elvin Edwards. This trolley was called the "Fisherman's Delight."

The South Shore Yacht Club opened in 1908 on the west side of Randall Bay. It was the social center for "all the wealth and fashion of Freeport." A large dining room, ball room, gymnasium, sleeping rooms, pool, and tennis courts were some of its amenities. The LIGHTS used it for many affairs before building a clubhouse. Guy Lombardo was a prominent member.

The Freeport Theater, located on Sunrise Highway, opened around 1922 as a vaudeville and movie house. It was constructed in the French Renaissance style. Made of white glazed terra-cotta, the theater offered 12 proscenium boxes and six mezzanine loges. It had large dressing rooms, an organ, and a cantilevered balcony. The orchestra pit accommodated 26 musicians. There were five movie projection machines and seats for 2,000 patrons.

The Grove Theatre was erected in 1926 on Merrick Road near Grove Street. It offered two daily shows of vaudeville and movies. Backstage, there was a large dressing room with a star on the door and eight other dressing rooms. The theater could accommodate a 21-piece orchestra. WGBB radio studios were located around the corner and would broadcast shows and interviews with performers.

The Sigmond Opera House opened in 1909 to an audience of 1,000. The building boasted a two-story front with an entrance in the shape of a horseshoe. Six dressing rooms were available for performers, and retiring rooms were located upstairs. The theater's interior was green and gold, and two boxes were located on either side of the stage. Situated on Main Street, it offered first-class vaudeville. It later became the American Theater but burned down on October 31, 1923.

The Plaza Theater was located on Grove Street, just south of the railroad, and was operated by Charles and Jennie Reitmeyer. In 1912, it was an open airdrome. Rebuilt and enlarged with a new pitched floor, heat, and a roof, it could seat nearly 300. The Plaza Theater was equipped for vaudeville as well as movie showings. Old-timers remember the building shaking when the train went by.

The War Camp Community Service Canteen used Schwab's Tavern on Olive Boulevard as a hospitality center for US soldiers and sailors during World War I. Each week between 1,000 and 2,000 servicemen were provided with relaxation and fun by more than 150 volunteers. Most of the servicemen came from Camp Mills in Garden City. A front room offered refreshments, while the canteen's west portion was a dance hall.

Lake Scene along Playland Park
Freeport, L.I.

Playland Park opened in 1924 on South Grove Street and Front Street on nine acres. The swimming facilities included the canal and a swimming pool. It included a huge scenic railway, Dodge 'Em and the Whip rides, a carousel, refreshment stands, games of chance, roller-skating, and a boxing ring. It was dubbed "the Coney Island of Long Island." The opening of Jones Beach and the Depression led to its demise. It burned down in 1931.

The Freeport Yacht Club was founded in the early 1930s by members of the Freeport Fire Department who desired a more reasonably priced club. Located on the Woodcleft Basin at the site of the old Playland Park, the Freeport Yacht Club had a most unusual clubhouse. Members utilized a large ship that had been a submarine tender for the US Navy. It had been towed from Oyster Bay.

Randall Park was donated to the village in 1924 as stipulated in John J. Randall's will. It was to be used as a public park and a high school recreation center, and no admission or usage fees could be charged. It is bounded by Cedar Street, South Grove Street, Ocean Avenue, and Front Street. When the Woodcleft Hotel was torn down, the property was added to the park.

The Freeport Golf Club was established in 1900 south of Merrick Road and west of Bayview Avenue. The 2,494-yard, nine-hole course was bounded by cedar trees. Randall and Miller built the clubhouse that featured a veranda, an assembly hall with cathedral-style windows, and a fireplace. Locker rooms were available for both men and women. Tournaments were held throughout the season. (MC.)

Seated in the pony cart is Bob Smalley, who was allegedly an outstanding sprinter in the very popular foot races at the turn of the 20th century. Among those in the rear are Hilbert Johnson, Hyman Schloss, and Lou DaSilva. In the back of the cart is Robert G. Anderson, meat market proprietor, who later became village president. The cart is parked in front of Conrader's Delicatessen.

In 1896, Raynor and Mott, from Freeport, opened the Greenhouse on Broad Channel for sportsmen and gunners. It was a fishing station on Hempstead Bay south of Bellmore. One of the first houses built, other than those on the beaches, it was the best-known station between Brooklyn and Montauk Point. Many local groups enjoyed the Greenhouse's hospitality.

BAYVIEW TENNIS COURTS, FREEPORT, L. I.

The Bayview Tennis Club, located between Locust Avenue and Elliott Place on Rose Street, featured five doubles courts and one singles court. Membership was limited to 150 men, 100 women, and 100 juniors. Teams were chosen, and tournaments were played with other tennis clubs on the south shore. Merritt Cutler was a member of one of the Bayview Tennis Club's teams.

The Grove Park Hotel opened in 1900 and could accommodate 150 guests. Located in a grove of tall oaks on Rose Street, it featured large piazzas, a dining room, suites with bathrooms, cottages, and a tennis court. It was built and operated by Owen Humphrey. Also known as the Imperial Hotel and the South Shore Apartments, it is still in existence in 2011.

The Crystal Lake Hotel and Cottage was built by Owen Humphrey in 1899 to accommodate 150 guests. A family hotel, it offered boating, bathing, fishing, and golf. Located on the northwest corner of South Grove Street and Southside Avenue, it once fronted Crystal Lake. It later became the Shorecrest and burned down in 1958. Seated on the front steps are Ward Frost Jr. and his family, the proprietors. (WF)

The Woodcleft Inn faced Front Street at the head of Woodcleft Canal. It was built in 1897 to house 200 guests. It was constructed by Randall and Miller for summer guests. It eventually became a Catholic orphanage maintained by the St. Vincent DePaul Society. They provided summer vacations to poor children and operated until 1921. In the early 1940s, Freeport village purchased the structure to enlarge Randall Park.

Hempstead Bay Yacht Club, Freeport, L. I.

The Hempstead Bay Yacht Club was located on Elder (Alder) Island at the turn of the 20th century and was accessible only by boat. It was considered the yachting crown jewel of the south shore. Many Freeport members were real estate agents who were giving out memberships to encourage house sales. In 1904, when the majority of the yacht club membership objected to this practice, the Freeporters resigned and pledged to build their own yacht club.

Baldwin Country Club, Baldwin, L. I., N. Y.

The Milburn Country Club was developed in the northwest section next to Milburn Creek from Stearns Park to Grand Avenue. In 1916, a group of New York City men met with Hugo Stearns, the owner. They offered to buy the land for a country club, and by early 1917, the group undertook the construction of a clubhouse, golf course, and tennis courts. (BHS.)

Freeport Lodge of Elks No. 1253 opened in 1912 in a house located at the southeast corner of Merrick Road and Grove Street. The first exalted ruler was J. Huyler Ellison. Because membership grew so rapidly, an addition was built in 1914. Eventually, the membership exceeded 1,000, and the Elks decided to sell the building and purchase a new site.

Ground was broken in 1924 for the Elks' new building. Formal dedication ceremonies were held on George Washington's birthday in 1926. The building was located on the Bergen family site on Merrick Road, just south of Bergen Place. It was a massive building with impressive two-story columns. The first floor contained a bar, dining room, and kitchen. Additionally, there were bowling alleys in the basement.

The Freeport Club was a men's social organization, and William P. Miller was its first president. In 1903, the clubhouse was constructed on Grove Street south of the railroad. The main floor had a reception hall, library, and dining room; the basement was used as a bowling alley. A large meeting hall was located on the second floor. The building became the Spartan Masonic Lodge in 1921.

The Freeport Field Club was a pioneer semiprofessional football team that rolled up about 60 consecutive victories from 1920 through 1927. It was Long Island's only semiprofessional gridiron aggregation east of Jamaica. In 1923, the players were, from left to right, (first row, kneeling) Art Jenkins, ? Canalizo, C. Smith, Herb Mahnken, ? Spence, ? Mitchell, Clinton Egan, ? Jaffe, Peter Kelly, and Peter Hansen; (second row, standing) H. Polette, C. Vollmer, G. Firth, ? Schlegel, C. Moyer, coach Mac, ? Doherty, Peck Bedell, B. Smith, C. Harris, and referee Rhodes.

114

Nine

BUSINESS COMMUNITY

Thomas W. Murray's Grove Parking & Service Station, a Socony gas station, was located west of the Grove Theatre. As a promotion, three elephants are standing at the station. A sign advertises gasoline for 16¢ per gallon.

Henry Schluter's grocery store was located at 33 West Merrick Road at the southeast corner of Church Street and Merrick Road. It offered delivery service, and its trademark was two white horses that doubled as fire horses to pull the fire truck at Hose Company No. 1, which was located around the corner. Schluter is to the left.

Antonio "Tony" Elar (1869–1934) ran a saloon and hotel on the north side of East Merrick Road around 1896. He and his family lived on the second floor and also took in boarders. In 1907, a fire started in the barroom of this neighborhood bar, and the building burned down. It was replaced by a large, brick hotel.

The Columbian Bronze Company was founded in 1900 on Atlantic Avenue and moved to North Main Street in 1911. Taking advantage of the marine trade in Freeport, the plant was devoted to making propellers. These propellers ranged in size from several inches to 10 feet in diameter. The company's slogan was "with a Columbian propeller behind you will come out ahead in the end." It closed in 1988.

The Review Building was located at 64 South Main Street (c. 1917). Charles D. Smith established the *Queens County Review* in Freeport in November 1895. Upon the separation of the County of Nassau from Queens, the title was changed to the *Nassau County Review* and was purchased by Smith F. Pearsall. The paper shared the building with the Long Island Cigar Store and Kiefer's Stationery store.

Early in the 20th century, the New York Telephone Company established a presence in Freeport. The new building was located on the west side of South Grove Street, just south of the Freeport Club. Employees are seen standing in the doorway. The sign in the window offers contracts and collections. Next door, to the right at 24 South Grove Street, is the office of William G. Miller and his son Raymond J. Miller.

Ira L'Hommedieu's building in 1911 was on the southeast corner of Merrick Road and Main Street. The 119–123 South Main Street edifice is sometimes referred to as the first strip mall. The confectionery store to the left was run by John Birkholz, and the middle section was occupied by Henry and Leopold Himmel's bakery. They bought the store from L'Hommedieu and renamed it the OK Bakery.

Albert and Arthur Heinrich were "pioneer builders of flying machines" and located their airplane factory at 50–60 East Merrick Road in 1916. They won a large government contract from the War Department to build planes. In 1910, the brothers from Baldwin flew the first American-made, American-powered monoplane. In 1916, Arthur flew one of the lightest hydroplanes in use. (CA.)

The Freeport Airport, located on 70 acres on South Grove Street, south of Playland Park, consisted of two grass-dirt runways, 1,500 and 200 feet long, and a hangar. During the 1928 dedication ceremonies, Elinor Smith arrived in her Sterner plane making the first landing. Pictured is an Alexander Eaglerock plane. The Depression led to its closure, and the land was sold off for housing. (CA.)

The four-story, redbrick Olive Building ran 60 feet on Main Street and 125 feet on Olive Boulevard. Jacob Post, a developer, built it and named it after his daughter Olive Post Smith (1903–1993). Work started on it about 1911, which included installing an elevator and bowling alleys in the basement. The tower on the roof adds an interesting architectural element. Stores and offices were the tenants.

The village's pioneer bank was the Freeport Bank, which was established in 1892. The first building was erected in 1905 at 24 South Main Street, just south of the railroad tracks. John J. Randall was president, and William S. Hall was cashier. Many prominent Freeporters were officers including Smith Cox, William G. Miller, and William Golder. Miller was the builder and used Indiana limestone and Roman bricks.

To the left is the original two-story First National Bank that opened in 1911. It was constructed of Indiana limestone after the Romanesque style, ornamented with Ionic Columbian pilasters. A unique way to keep the bank open was to build the new one to the east of the original one. Upon completion, the old building was demolished.

The First National Bank and Trust Company was completed in 1929. The Art Deco, flatiron-style bank featured six stories with a two-story base. The base was of granite and topped by two stories of limestone and brick, with limestone trim above. Mayan reliefs are on the facade of the building. The lobby was finished in Caen stone marble and bronze, replete with an elevator, cigar stand, mail chute, and staircase.

The Freeport Bank grew quickly and needed additional space. In 1925, a new bank was erected just south of the original on the corner of Olive Boulevard and South Main Street. The architects were Purdy and Davis, and Rufus Brown Co. was the builder. D. Wesley Pine was the president. At the time, "it was declared the most modern, up-to-date banking institution in Nassau County."

The Freeport Hotel was located on Main Street, just south of the railroad tracks. Established in 1881, the original building was wooden clapboard with wide porches. It was owned by the Benson Smith family. In 1909, it was replaced by a two-story brick building. Euterpean Hall was located on the second floor to accommodate entertainment and banquets. The hotel suffered a major fire in the 1950s and was torn down when the railroad was elevated.

When Chester Fulton came to Freeport in 1904, he bought a farm on Church Street near Merrick Road. The two children in front are his son Curtis and his adopted daughter Jennie Pace. His wife was Cecelia Guedon. To the left is Henry Ryder, who was later with the Freeport police and fire departments.

Theodore Bedell, left, had his blacksmith shop at 109 Church Street dating back to 1894. There, he shoed horses and performed oxy-acetylene work and cast-iron welding. He also worked on cab tops and truck bodies. He invented a unique folding anchor for small vessels. He also built fire wagons for the Oceanside and Rockville Centre Fire Departments. Despite this variety of work, he called himself the "practical horse shoer."

There were a number of retail establishments on Brooklyn Avenue just north of the Long Island Rail Road tracks and west of Main Street. They included a tailor; H.W. Theel, electrical contractor; Mook Laundry; a real estate office; T.A. Wright Plumbing and Heating; and the "tugboat" building. A sign states that the John J. Randall Company moved to Long Beach Avenue.

The Realty Building was also known as the Otten and the Hub Building. Located on the corner of Church Street and Railroad Avenue, it contained offices of some of the most influential businessmen in Freeport, including George Morton Levy. Mechanics' Hall was available for the meetings of various organizations, including the Elks, Masons, and Daughters of Liberty. On the ground floor was Schiller's Bar, a hangout for actors.

Charles P. Smith (1871–1965) opened a drugstore at the intersection of Main Street and Church Street around 1890. It had a beautiful flower garden at the point of its triangular grounds, formerly occupied by the first schoolhouse. Persons waiting for the trolley kept warm in his store. He formed a partnership with Charles W. Bedell and introduced new features like an ice cream counter and medical equipment.

William Foreman (1847–1896) and his son C. Milton Foreman (1875–1955) owned Foreman's Hardware, two lumberyards, and a considerable amount of residential property. The original planing mill and lumberyard was located on the south side of Atlantic Avenue near South Main Street. Foreman moved the business to Commercial Street near the railroad tracks. It burned down in a spectacular fire in 1953.

1908

George Bennett Smith started selling bicycles in 1896 and, later, ran a Model T Ford and a Cadillac agency on the northwest corner of Merrick Road and Henry Street. By 1927, he owned a large garage located behind the main building, where he pumped gas, had a machine shop, a repair department, a body and paint shop, and a tire shop. Smith owned the first automobile in Freeport, a runabout. (KA.)

Radio station WGBB was Long Island's first commercial radio station. It was owned and managed by Harry H. Carman, who went on the air commercially on December 13, 1923. The original studio was set up in Carman's father's garage (pictured) at 217 Bedell Street adjacent to the transmitter. After obtaining a commercial license, Carman located the first studio at 66 South Grove Street.

BIBLIOGRAPHY

Bermudez, Miguel, and Donald Giordano. *An Illustrated History of Freeport Fire Department, 1893–2008*. Freeport, NY: Freeport Fire Department, 2008.

DeLorme, John F. *A Pictorial History of Early Freeport, NY*. Freeport, NY: 1955.

Freeport Long Island Illustrated. Freeport, NY: c. 1907.

Freeport Past and Present: With a Prospect of Its Future. Freeport, NY: Freeport Methodist Church, 1900.

Hager, Fred, and Isabelle Drach. *Freeport, It's a Wonderful Town*. Freeport, NY: self-published, 1995.

Hazelton, Henry Isham. *The Boroughs of Brooklyn and Queens, Counties of Nassau Suffolk, Long Island, New York, 1609–1924*. NY: Lewis Historical Publishing Company, Inc., 1925.

Johnson, Hilbert R. *Freeport, Its History and Progress*. Freeport, NY: Freeport Unemployment Relief Committee, 1934.

Metz, Clinton W. *Freeport As It Was*. Freeport, NY: self-published, 1976.

Smith, Elinor. *Aviatrix*. NY: Harcourt Brace Jovanovich, 1981.

Tredwell, Daniel M. *Personal Reminiscences of Men and Things on Long Island*. Brooklyn, NY: C.A. Ditmas, 1912–1917.

www.freeportlihistory.blogspot.com

www.longislandmemories.org

Visit us at
arcadiapublishing.com